D1512202

like a man gone mad

OTHER WORKS BY SAMUEL HAZO

POETRY

The Song of the Horse
A Flight to Elsewhere
Just Once
As They Sail
The Holy Surprise of Right Now
Silence Spoken Here
Nightwords
The Color of Reluctance
Thank a Bored Angel
To Paris
Quartered
Once for the Last Bandit
Twelve Poems
Blood Rights
My Sons in God
Listen with the Eye
The Quiet Wars
Discovery

FICTION

This Part of the World
Stills
The Wanton Summer Air
The Very Fall of the Sun
Inscripts

CRITICISM

Smithereened Apart:
    A Critique of Hart Crane

ESSAYS

The Autobiographers of Everybody
The Power of Less
The Pittsburgh That Stays Within You
The Feast of Icarus
The Rest Is Prose
Spying for God

PLAYS

Watching Fire, Watching Rain
Mano A Mano: A Flamenco Drama
    (The Life of Manolete)
Feather
Solos
Until I'm Not Here Anymore

like
a man
gone
mad

Poems in a New Century

Samuel Hazo

Syracuse University Press

∞ The paper used in this publication meets the minimum requirements of the American National Standard for Information Sciences—Permanence of Paper for Printed Library Materials, ANSI Z39.48-1992.

For a listing of books published and distributed by Syracuse University Press, visit our Web site at SyracuseUniversityPress.syr.edu.

The author wishes to express special thanks to his copy editor Julie DuSablon.

ISBN 978-0-8156-0957-5

Library of Congress Cataloging-in-Publication Data

Hazo, Samuel John.
    Like a man gone mad : poems in a new century / Samuel Hazo. — 1st ed.
        p. cm.
    ISBN 978-0-8156-0957-5 (cloth : alk. paper)
    I. Title.
    PS3515.A9877L55 2010
    811'.54—dc22   2010035078

Manufactured in the United States of America

For Sam and Anna and Sarah

Odd that a thing is most itself
when likened.

Richard Wilbur

Caminante, son tus huellas
el camino, y nada más;
caminante, no hay camino,
se hace camino el andar.

Antonio Machado

Action is once; the word is forever.

Adonis

The author of more than thirty books of poetry, fiction, essays, and plays, SAMUEL HAZO is the founder and director of the International Poetry Forum in Pittsburgh, Pennsylvania. He is also McAnulty Distinguished Professor of English Emeritus at Duquesne University. From 1950 to 1957 he served in the United States Marine Corps, completing his tour as a captain. He was graduated magna cum laude from the University of Notre Dame and received his master's degree from Duquesne University and his doctorate from the University of Pittsburgh. Some of his most recent books are *The Song of the Horse* (poetry), *This Part of the World* (fiction), *The Power of Less* (essays), and *Watching Fire, Watching Rain* (drama). He has also translated essays by Denis de Rougemont and the poems of Adonis and Nadia Tueni. His book of poems, *Just Once: New And Previous Poems*, received the Maurice English Poetry Award in 2003. The University of Notre Dame, from which he received the Griffin Award for Creative Writing in 2005 and which will publish *The Stroke of a Pen: Essays on Poetry and Other Provocations* in 2011, awarded him his tenth honorary doctorate in 2008. A National Book Award finalist, he was chosen the first State Poet of the Commonwealth of Pennsylvania by Governor Robert Casey in 1993, and he served until 2003.

Contents

Acknowledgments

Some of the poems in this book appeared originally in the *Hopkins Review*, the *Hudson Review*, the *Sewanee Review*, *Provincetown Arts Journal*, *Salmagundi*, *Four Rivers Review*, *Inclined to Speak*, *The Other Side of Sorrow*, and the *Pittsburgh Post-Gazette*. "Home Are the Sailors" is the spoken section of a musical composition by my son, Samuel Robert Hazo. It was given its world premier in Carnegie Hall in New York by the Notre Dame Symphony Orchestra on May 11, 2010.

like a man gone mad

To the Next Poem

I trust you to say everything
    I know but never know
    I know until I write it.
I trust you to be born
    when due but not a second
    before.
           Your birth will be
    as always breech—an ordeal
    of hours, luck and anguish.
I trust you to be difficult
    but not impossible.
               I trust you
    as a dog trusts his nose.
I trust you more than fathers
    trust their sons, or brothers
    their brothers since truth at last
    is truer than blood.
              I trust you
    to be sudden as redemption or defeat.
Since pressure doubles when volume
    shrinks, I trust you to confirm
    that poems are compressed intensities.
I trust you to be unforgettably
    the first and last and only.

1

Briefly in Attendance

Once, Again

Each April is the same
   but somehow greener every year.
Lovers who've made love
   on hundreds of nights anticipate
   the next loving as their first.
Shaving for the twenty-seven
   thousandth time on the Fourth
   of another July should be
   no different, but it is.
                              Breakfast
   today, although identical
   with yesterday's, is one day
   better.
            Even these words
   have predecessors by the millions
   from my very hand, but still
   I write them as the first
   and final words I'll write.
Some say I should be bored.
If so, I should be bored
   with breathing, but I'm not.
If you believe hereafter's
   here already, and that now
   is always now, you'd say
   the same.
               And you'd be right.

Sudden or Slow but Sure

Wounded by shrapnel in France
   six decades back, he's still
   recovering from trauma caused
   by trauma.
            In every book
by Edward Wood he resurrects
the pain.
            When Hemingway received
the wound that made him think
at Fassalta di Piave, the outcome
was the same: reliving
and retelling what was sudden,
merciless and permanent.
                It's not
confined to war.
            Preparing
for a trip to Europe, Reynolds
Price complained of cramping
in his lower back.
            X-rays
confirmed a shadow.
            Days
later he awoke from surgery
a paraplegic.
            Shock was the first
response, then transformation.
                Bernard
Costello cased his saxophone
to specialize in oral surgery
after his dearest friend
was mangled in a crash.

H. R.

survived a stroke but lived
a posthumous existence to the end.
And there was Frank the catcher.
Built like a heavyweight, he stood
    akimbo when he spoke, flexing
    his jaw as if each word
    were like a throw to second.
First-string at twenty on the college
    varsity, he'd been approached
    by scouts and was inclined.
Struck later in the jaw
    by a ball thrown wild and hard,
    he changed.
                Thirty pounds
    lighter with a wired jawbone
    and six teeth lost, he seemed
    uncertain to the point of deference.
The list has no amen.
                To trump
    the odds, discretion matters less
    than valor, which matters less
    than zero where absurdity's concerned.
The ultimate defense is luck.
The ultimate reprieve is luck.

The Contrarians

On the one hand, cure—
   the hopes and risks of cure.
Otherwise, predictable pain—
   ongoing, sudden or ultimate.
Only a masochist would opt
   for pain—and a strong masochist
   at that.
        But what if cure
   becomes a lesser or even
   worse choice than pain?
Griffin, the diabetic, learned
   that amputation of one leg
   would add a decade to his life.
"Forget the years," he said,
   "I'd rather die—entire . . ."
Knowing she had to drive him
   ninety miles for dialysis
   thrice weekly, Sigmund decided
   it was time.
        The drive was aging
   Jane, and all for what?
One night he said, "Enough's
   enough," and then he kissed her.
For eight more days they were
   closer than ever . . .
        Trapped
   high in the South Tower
   with no way down or up
   and fire and smoke behind,
   they held each other's hands
   like newlyweds a hundred

floors above Manhattan
in September and jumped . . .
To those who say survival
is the highest law of life,
I offer the above.
                    Plus one . . .
Soldiers have risked or sacrificed
their lives to save the lives
of men they could have just
let die.
            Call theirs an act
of greater love or call it
anything you please.
                    To all
who claim that life amounts
to nothing more than not dying,
I say there are exceptions.

"Are There Poets Any More?"

I said there were, but are there?
The student who asked if poets
   had vanished from the earth like Vikings
   had a point.
           Apart from all
   the workshop gangs, the blurb
   exchangers and the buddy-buddy
   cliques, what's left?
              A name
or two, and that's the norm.
Few giants.
           But then has Shakespeare
   had an equal earlier or since?
I asked that very student
   to describe what poetry meant.
"It's putting your best words
   together with feelings in them."
Another point.
           It bested Eliot
   by stressing feelings, which Eliot
   the critic left unmentioned.
A further point.
           If all
   the poetry the student read
   was word design or language flattened
   into sociology like yard goods,
   who could fault him?
             Someone
   suggested Whitman as a cure.
I had my doubts since Whitman's
   laundry lists of itemized

Americana glut the mind.
Poems are meant to peak,
    not sprawl.
                And all the rhymesters
    now in vogue will matter less.
They'll end like old unhappy
    women matching miseries
    to gauge who's been ignored
    or unappreciated most.
                        Of those
    above the herd from Plymouth Rock
    to now, I favor eight.
I won't name names.
                Why start
    an argument?
                Unlike the vanished
    Vikings, poets will last as long
    as people last but never
    on demand and rarely in abundance.

Aesop Revisited

Why is it I favor snow
   and rain when all they do
   is slow things down?
                  Is slowness
   itself the reason why
   since only then can poems
   be written, needles threaded
   and kisses given as they should be—
   free of calculation and with eyes
   lidded?
          Slowed down or stopped
   completely to observe a waterfall,
   I learn to share the happy
   recklessness of water on the run.
I'm prompted then to say how men
   of thought look noblest
   when they read or vote or pray
   or listen to Sibelius alone . . .
The hare arrives fatigued
   with nothing showing for his speed
   except the vanity of victory.
The tortoise stops en route
   to view the scenery, forgets
   how far he's come or has
   to go and then resumes the rivalry
   like some unlikely hero
   barely winded from the trek
   and yet to break a sweat.

The Fifth Element

Three we find as given.
One we make.
                    And the fifth?
The fifth presents a problem.
The earth is waiting to be tamed,
    seeded, tunneled or plowed.
Water is ours for drinking,
    bathing, cooking or sailing.
The air makes vassals of us all,
    and fire will kindle on demand
    from nothing into flame and ash.
But clouds?
                    As spume or spray
or white ascensions billowing
through space or thunderheads
as sudden as volcanic smoke,
they hug the world like works
in progress.
                    What's happening beneath
repeats the travesty called history:
genocide in Africa, soldieries
drugged by uniforms and slogans,
governments ruled by democratically
elected undermen or thugs.
The clouds slur over them
    indifferently.
                    Surnamed in Latin
as cumulus, nimbus, cirrus
and stratus, they even sound
like facts in motion.

And that's
their secret.
Mountains arise
in place and stay there.
Rivers
surrender to the sea and never
leave.
Fires that flare
and blaze into infernos rarely
last for long.
And what
is air but mere transparency?
But clouds create themselves
in pilgrimage and never twice
the same.
They shadow all
they cover and are gone.
Like all
the best of guests, they're briefly
in attendance.
They keep their proper
distance, hover and move on.

Prognosticators and Other Distractions

I have news for you.
                    Predicting
that tomorrow's happened long before
it's even here is like remembering
ahead of time.
                    By definition
prophesying means to see
and say what's happening.
                         Although
the present must become the past
before it's understandable, if then,
we crave the comfort of such wisdom
in advance.
                    Driving near Abilene,
I heard a radio evangelist
predict the world would end
in seven days.
                    Thousands
believed though nothing happened
on the seventh day or after.
                         They loved
his certitude and overlooked
the faulty math . . .
                    In training
once I had to ford at midnight
with a rifle and full pack
a stream in flood.
                    Water
battered boulders, and the sky
was two dim stars.

                    I stepped
in darkness like a hooded sailor
walking the plank.
                    Halfway
across . . .
                Why bother saying
how it ended?
                    All you
who think that endings are conclusions,
think again.
                Conclusions show
what endings mean, which leaves you
stalled with me alone
at midnight in midstream in mid-thought
and certain only that's uncertainty
is all that's certain as we go.

In Troth

Forget the birthdays.
                    For me
    you're younger than ever.
                              Nothing
    is truer than that.
                    Tonight
    I thought of life without you,
    and I died—no one to kid
    or kiss, no one to say
    that blue is not my color,
    no one to shuck mussels with
    from the same bowl, no one
    to live the patience that is love
    in waiting.
                You're always new
    to know—a mate I choose
    all over every day.
                    You make
    our lives seem one long day
    with no past tense.
                    I love you
    for the times you've slowed me down
    before I would have blundered.
I love you for the hundred ways
    you saw what I would
    never see until you'd seen it
    first.
            We're nip and tuck,
    saddle and boot, a pair
    of gloves, a study in rhyme

from A to Z without a flub
between.
          We're grateful so
for one lone son whose music
loops the globe, grandchildren
three, and Dawn who keeps
all five in love together
and intact.
              If I could make
right now eternal as a song,
I would.
             Impossible, of course.
But not the wanting to . . .
                   That's why
I want impossibility to last,
regardless.
             That's happiness.

2

Not a Soul Applauds

Making It Look Easy

Whatever it is, Spencer Tracy
   had it—acting as if he wasn't
   acting, which is acting at its best.
So did Fred Astaire and Ginger Rogers
   swirling in "The Continental," Bojangles
   tapping, Michael Jackson
   at his peak, Nureyev leaping
   and Gene Kelly on his own.
Sampras in his prime made sport
   and grace synonymous.
                    Seferis
in Beirut preserved within himself
the Greece the Nazis never
could defeat.
             Greece lives forever
and wherever in his poetry.
                   And that's
the point.
         There's one Seferis
to a century, if that.
              The same
is true of those named
heretofore who made a poem
of their work.
            Why bother with less
when nothing better than the best
should ever be imagined?
                Let those
who say that poetry is mere
technique be damned.

They're thinking
only of the tricks that inspiration
nixes with impunity to let
perfection happen . . .
                    I had
an uncle who was tops in pool.
No one could match him.
                    Thirty
years retired from the game,
he took a pool shark's challenge
as a dare.
            Without a session
to rehearse, he chalked his cue,
then broke the rack and ran
the table as of old.
                    The bet
was made and paid, and that
was that.
            Even the loser
was amazed to watch a master
show him how poetically
the art of 8-ball could be played.

The Short Life of Perpetuity

Amin Maalouf could write:
   "Our sole consolation, before
   being laid to rest, is to have loved
   and been loved, and perhaps
   to have left a personal trace."
Commendable, of course.
                    Not quite
   as slick as a lyric by Cole
   Porter but basically true.
Translated, it means how all
   that's once and only supercedes
   what pleases in passing but never
   fulfills.
            And I agree.
Show me whoever balks
   at being loved or loving back,
   I'll show you a fool.
               But what's
 "a personal trace?"
              For men
it might be hoping to be profiled
on a coin or stamp or having airports,
parks or boulevards perpetuate
their names.
            Most women
could care less.
             For them to know
that those most dear to them
are well and happy is memorial
enough.

They see the rest
as vanity or rational stupidity.
If moments lived are not
their own reward, then what's
the point?
                    Clark Gable
knew the difference.
                        Idolized
by millions in his prime, he spoke
dismissively of stardom—"I eat
and use the bathroom like everybody."
When asked what kind of funeral
he'd want, he snorted, "Don't make
a circus out of it."
                        Recently
I asked a group of undergraduates
if they remembered Clark Gable.
None did except one girl who said,
"I think I've heard the name."
Gable would have smiled at that.

Targets

When Johnson took him on a hunt
   for deer in Texas, Kennedy
   declined the rifle with a grin.
And that said something of the man.
Each time I pass a roadkill
   or an antlered stag spread-eagled
   on the tailgate of a truck, I realize
   that some see deer as so much
   venison—or carriers of lyme
   disease—or varmints too destructive
   to be spared.
           But there's a grace
   about them when they graze and feed
   and leap that eases me.
               Then history
intrudes.
        It shows how man
the farmer-healer-teacher
   superseded man the hunter,
   but the hunter in him never dies.
It leaves him prone to kill.
From sport to war is not
   too far a leap for those
   who think of warfare as a sport
   where men are targeted as so much
   meat.
       Men's flesh and deer pelt
   bleed the same.

The will behind
the aim that finds it laudable
to kill makes death the reason
for the game.
Bullets are blind.

Kennedy

I came before they built
  the monument, and what I saw
  was scarcely monumental: sloped
  grass on either shoulder
  of the road that curved and banked
  below an overpass, the book building
  overlooking ordinary traffic
  patterns on an ordinary Friday
  of an ordinary March, the skyline
  clouding ordinarily to rain . . .
One shot missed, but two
  hit, according to reports.
Cheap rifle, moving target,
  lone shooter firing down,
  re-aiming twice—the facts
  defied ballistics and belief.
Later I saw post mortem
  photos of a face unmarked
  by exit wounds or evidence
  of impact.
              Questions, controversy,
  suppositions . . .
              Following his route,
  I passed a billboard opposite
  the first trajectory.
              An ordinary
  billboard.
              That must have been
  the final thing he saw.

The Fools of God

If certain politicians come
  across as serious jokes,
  what's left for you to do
  but say so while you frown
  and laugh?
               Not that it changes
anything, but then who knows?
At worst it lets you add
  some further cautions to your creeds.
On poetry, carpentry, dance
  and sports—the art is not
  to show the art.
             On help—
too much too soon, too little
too late.
        On destiny—life
matters more than death
since life's explorable while death's
unknowable and final.
              On weapons—
gun owners should be forced
by law to learn to play
the violin.
        On money—what's earned
is truer than what's gifted or won
by luck.
      On fate—all
that we learn in retrospect
is worthless in the present tense.
Call these the credos of a fool
  in any commonwealth whose only

gods are acquisition or celebrity,
and you'd be right.
                    Regardless,
when courage or conformity are all
the options left, most fools
courageously disdain conformity
and dare to face the odds.
That's why they're fools to everyone
except themselves.
                    They know
they're closest to the truth
when what they say arouses
mockery while not a soul applauds.

The Merchandiser's Song

Sell only the best for as much as you can
and make it appear like a bargain from God.
It takes as much work to sell rubies as toothpicks,
but watch how the difference quintuples your profits
and let that convince you the difference is worth it.
I've done this for years so I know what I'm saying.

It's true that men buy, but smart women shop,
which means that they notice while men merely look.
When choosing a car, a woman will favor
a color that makes it the key to the deal,
and the man has no choice but to buy it to please her.
I've dealt with all kinds so I know what I'm saying.

With Arabs you haggle, with Brits you're exact.
Don't deal with Chinese, or you're certain to lose.
A Frenchman in business is cold but correct.
A Spaniard stays calm unless he feels cheated,
but if he feels cheated, you better leave town.
I've traveled a lot so I know what I'm saying.

Don't brag of your gains, or you'll gain the wrong friends.
When you lose, you'd be wise not to mention your losses.
Gripe, and you'll find that you bore your defenders
and gladden all those who were happy you flopped.
Look up when you're down, look down when you're up.
I've lost and I've won so I know what I'm saying.

If men need to choose for today or tomorrow,
they'll choose for today, and tomorrow can wait.
This means that you sell them what tempts them right now

before they can muster a reason to tell you
they would if they could or thanks, but no thanks.
I've learned how men think so I know what I'm saying.

Selling yourself is a game without mercy.
If nobody buys, you're equal to zero.
The name of the game is how much you are worth.
If you make a million, you're worth what you've made.
If you take in nothing, you're not worth a thing.
I've sold my whole life so I know what I'm saying.

Sloth Is the Mother of Invention

Because he tired of climbing stairs,
    Otis invented elevators
    which invented skyscrapers
    which converted downtown Chicago,
    Dallas and New York into downtown
    Chicago, Dallas and New York . . .
Intrigued with automobility,
    Henry Ford produced the horseless
    carriage that promoted sanitation
    plus convenience.
                    No more manure
    on city streets.
                 More speed,
    less shoveling.
                 Stench became
a memory, and people drove
while sitting statue-still behind
a wheel . . .
                 Plumbing and flushable
commodes made dumping chamber
pots defunct while buttoned
or zippered trouser-flies for men
and skirts for women sensibly
facilitated urination . . .
                 Dismissive
of negotiations and slow wars,
    Hitler simply blitzed his enemies.
If might made right, why bother
    with diplomacy?
                 Diplomacy took time,
and time took effort, and effort

meant time wasted if war
could cut the time in half . . .
Show me a shortcut, and I'll prove
how only people steeped
in laziness could give us elevators—
autos—toilets—clothing
tailored for hygiene—and war
and be proclaimed, for good
or ill or both, ingenious.

3

The Way It Is

Blossom

I sing of Blossom in her proud
    and permanent prime.
                      She celebrates
    one hundred and three birthdays
    by wearing crimson lipstick
    and designer eyewear à la Gucci.
She's had her white hair bobbed
    beneath a crowning scarf.
She's totally lost count of every
    President she voted for, outlived
    and left to history.
                      In photographs
she smiles with all her original
teeth.
           Dismissive of dotage,
she chooses wardrobes that are right
for her and her alone,
as in her preference for lingerie
a generation east of Mae West.
She leaves no room for doubt.
After her oldest daughter
    mentioned that she'd changed her will,
    Blossom asked her with a smile,
    "What did you leave me?"

Welcome to Used-to-Was

After you pass the Orthodontic
   Center near the Chrysler dealership,
   you'll see an Apostolic Church
   between two blocks of Civil War
   frame houses with flags
   a-flutter from every porch,
   a neon sign that welcomes
   hunters, and all that's left
   of an old Sunoco station
   gone to weeds and desolation
   near a second Apostolic Church
   that used to be a clinic
   for sick dogs.
                         The locals call
   this village Used-to-Was because
   the way it is is not
   the way it was.
                         Storefronts
   are boarded up for sale or rent
   except for one that offers
   cigarettes, cold beer and porn,
   an office selling bail bonds
   by appointment, and markets hawking
   shooting duds for hunters in deer
   season.
                 The highway leading
   into town becomes Main Street,
   which has the same three stoplights
   that it's had since the Depression.

If all the lights are green
   your next time by, it takes
   two minutes—plus or minus—
   and you're in and through and out.

Tattoos

They once were seen as trademarks
  of distinction for sailors.
                Lately
  they're everywhere you look.
For men—lightning zigzags
  on the ankles, deltas of Venus
  where chin meets chest, American
  flags on shoulder blades or cocks.
For women—a blue and smiling
  moon sequestered in the small
  of the back, roses on the upper
  ass, a Christian cross
  between the breasts, or an arrow
  pointing southward from the navel.
Cannibals believed tattoos
  distinguished them from beasts.
But now who knows if each
  tattoo's a badge or just
  graffiti with an attitude?
                Some
  call it body art.
            Some say
  it's ink on meat.
           If no
erasing laser's in the cards,
it's there for keeps, which means
it's guaranteed to last for life
and in the grave.
           It never sleeps.

The King of Swing

They tromp on stage in fours
    with amplified guitars low slung
    and aimed at fans who clap
    and yelp and ought to know
better.
        Add flashing lights
    and smoke, and there's the formula.
What's total din for me
    is ecstasy for them, and tens
    of thousands pay to hear it . . .
Give me the years of Benny
    Goodman in his prime.
                                    I
    saw him twice but loved
    his music long before
    I saw him once: Krupa
    on drums, Hampton on vibes
    and Teddy Wilson on piano.
To show he could, he guested
    with the Philharmonic and performed
    the Paganini variations to a tee.
The night I saw him last
    he let the spotlight stay
    on Ziggy Elman's trumpet
    dialogues with Krupa's paradiddles.
He listened like a king in shadow,
    snapping his fingers and tapping
    his toes.
            Watching him prime
    his clarinet and prep his reed,
    we waited like the amateurs we were

to hear the solo that we knew
would come.
       And when it came,
we heard a maestro in performance
at his best, unamplified and perfect.

Bring Back the Derby

Of all that ever crowned the head,
    the derby was the most distinctive—
    squatter than stovepipes, firmer
    than fedoras, dressier than caps,
    berets or tam-o'-shanters.
                    What else
    could make a tramp in rags
    look elegant?
           Or hut the body's
    rising warmth within a brimmed,
    inverted bowl that otherwise
    would dissipate like vapor in the wind?
It flourished in the age of spats,
    but now both it and spats
    are memories.
           But why?
                 I know
    that tastes keep changing
    with the times, but change can stay
    unchanged or change again
    as readily as not.
           It just
    takes someone who's admired
    and conspicuous to take a stand
    and start a trend.
           It worked
for the inventor of the wheel.
                It worked
for Christ.
          It worked for any
revolutionary you can name.

What
happened once can happen twice.
Tactics might have to change,
but strategy could stay the same.

Marrying My Shirt

Precisely and petitely folded,
  fastened by roundheaded pins
  at all the pleated points
  to keep the cuffs and collar
  shaped and propped and plumped,
  it waits in silence like a bride.
There's something virginal here.
Sleeved in cellophane, it prompts me
  to abandon it to its repose
  in recognition of the care that someone
  in Malaysia took to pack it.
But even admiration has
  its limits, so I free it
  from display like anything that's packaged
  for a purpose.
            One by one,
  I pluck six pinheads
  from their posts, release the plastic
  uprights underneath the collar,
  loosen buttons top to bottom
  and perform what every shirt invites.
I fill it with myself and make it
  freshly and immaculately mine.

Off and Running

It's yours as long as you accept it
    as a gift.
             But stifle it
with predetermined rhymes
or cadences, and what you have
is something less than poetry.
There's precedent enough to prove it.
Dancers are never dancers
    while they toe their marks or count
    their steps.
            It's not until
the music and the dancers mate
that dancing dances into dance.
Lorca likewise coined a name
    for *deepsong* when the blood is so
inflamed and frenzied that the singer
sings possessed.
           And finally
in football there's a time
when scrimmages release one
runner with a chance for momentary
fame.
        Dodging while he keeps
his feet to stay in play,
he sprints away from tackle
after tackle and creates before our eyes
the unexpected poem of the game.

Say Cheese

You force a smile until
    you think you look the way
    you think you look.
                The man
    behind the camera wants
    a bigger smile, and you comply
    as to a dentist's, "Open wider."
For smiles to qualify as smiles,
    the eyes and lips must rhyme,
    but now your eyes resign
    from the equation.
                Plain vanity
    sustains the shot, and authenticity
    be damned.
                You hold the pose.
Since posing is what posing
    does, you learn that all
    that posing does is mold you
    in a pose the poser wants.
For just that long, you're who
    you're not.
              When you unpose
    and are yourself again,
    you see what made the Iroquois
    believe that being photographed
    permitted the photographer to steal
    your soul.
              The Iroquois were right.

4

Louder in Silence

Sleep Is a Dangerous Exile

Watches, shoes and outer garb?
Superfluous.
                  Loose-fitting cottons
      will do or nothing at all,
      depending on the Fahrenheit.
Some claim that sleep's the ultimate
      democracy this side of death
      although it wastes one-third
      of every day and every life
      in deference to nothing but fatigue.
Asleep, you feel defenseless
      and alone.
                  Nightmares
      will stun you like a storm at sea,
      quicksand will suck you
      under, and the dead will rise.
It's more than Freudian suppression
      that's at work.
                        It's life's exact
      revenge upon itself, and you're
      the victim.
                  The lone escape
      is waking up.
                        You leave
      your dreams the way a swimmer
      leaves the ocean, no longer
      threatened by that element.
                              But dangers
      never die, and you will swim
      those depths again . . .

Remember
the swerving car that almost
ran you down?
It grazed you
like a passing curse and smeared
its fender salt like whitewash
on your coat.
An inch here,
an inch there . . .
But in your dreams
you're always hit.
Your coat's
entangled with a tire.
You're being
dragged and mangled by the wheels.
The driver speeds away
but not from guilt or fear
of being found at fault.
It seems
he never even saw you.

Skull Teeth

Bared and clenched, they summon
    images of grim equality
    or ghoulish glee.
                Despite
the skulls I've noticed photographed
    in Asian killing fields
    or stacked like stock in catacombs,
    I favor the equality of glee.
The grins of the unburied dead
    show us alike without disguise.
Caucasian?
            Oriental?
                  Who can tell?
What once was structure whitens
    like driftwood aging to finality
    or less.
            What some might see
as merely skeletal I see
as infrastructure and support
as long as we're supportable.
When everything else is past
    or withering to dust, our bones
    speak out to say we were
    who we were, and the teeth speak last.

Bold Old Scold

It's not that aging is predictable.
It's not.
        It more or less
just happens—recently *more*
rather than *less.*
            For instance,
you remember faces better than names,
which let themselves be known too late
or not at all.
            Your ears have quietly
embraced free will.
            They hear
the things they choose to hear.
Your knees are on sabbatical
    forever.
        To run, make love
or sleep uninterruptedly are nothing
now but problems to be solved,
which proves that living on amounts
to making do.
            Accidents,
disease or similar absurdities
may intervene, but where's the benefit
in that?
        They leave you cornered
like a man gone mad who stares
at those still cursed with sanity
and laughs and laughs to prove
the joke's on them.
            And it is.

A World with Nobody in It

A woman's voice instructed me
    to leave a message.
                    I hung up.
Later another voice recording,
    female and metallic as the first,
    informed me I'd been chosen for a prize.
I think I hung up also,
    but I can't (or won't) remember.
In town I pressed an elevator
    tab and smiled at my fellow
    passenger.
                "I never speak,"
    she hissed, "to strange men
    on elevators, sir."
                    I wondered
    what I would or could have done
    if she had screamed.
                        All day
    I spoke to no one else.
Shopping, I checked out all
    my groceries by credit card,
    refueled my car myself
    by credit card and ordered
    a takeout through a microphone.
Later I thumbed a button
    labeled *push* and parked in silence
    at an unattended lot, punched out
    in sequence the proper buttons
    to procure my airline ticket
    and on arrival rented a dolly
    from a rack to cart my bags.

Before I slept I realized
   I'd never really talked with anyone
   all day and never even
   needed to.
               But where's the life
   in that?
          Compare it to a pub
   in Galway or Kilkenny where the fare
   is song and talk and more talk.
Or the lot of mates in war
   where everybody shares alike.
Or the old and stricken who need
   the daily bread of company.
Or Steinbeck's ending in *The Grapes*
   of Wrath where a nursing mother
   feeds a starved and dying man
   the milk from her very body.

Heredity's a Card That's
Always Dealt Face Down

I met the daughter of a daughter
  of a student from an English class
  I offered fifty years ago.
Like someone overtaken in a race,
  I felt both in arrears and dated.
Appearing older with the young
  but younger with the old is how
  I see myself these days.
But what's the point?
                    Are years
  from birth more relevant than history?
I trace my mother's heritage
  to great grandparents only,
  and my father's to his father—
  no farther back than that.
My nameless predecessors vanish
  in Darwinian oblivion.
                          Or do they?
Whatever they were, I am.
Who knows what heathens, heroes,
  Homers, hookers, Hitlers,
  hunters, holier-than-thouers,
  hacks or hicks or humpbacks
  hide like secrets in my genes?
I'm just the next progenitor
  whose future is a past to come.
If that's the formula, why fret?

Between the randomly begotten
   and the soon to be forgotten,
   I expect I'll be remembered only
   as a temporary presence known
   as me and, even then, dismissively.

"Are You Sam Hazo's Grandfather?"

Including my late father,
    we are four plus a far
    distant cousin we've never met
    who have the same first
    and last name.
           At times
it's understandably confusing.
My wife will call one Sam,
    then hear a trio of answers.
Choosing the French and Spanish
    way of asking not your name
    but how you're called, we're nicknamed
    Sam, Sam-Sam and Sam A.
Apart from first and last
    names in common, we're not
    at all alike.
           Grandfather,
father and grandson qualify
    as wordsmith, maker of music
    for symphonic winds, and a pupil
    with yet unknown potential.
Sometimes we seem like runners
    in a relay passing off our name
    like a baton from life to life.
Since I'm the eldest, I can think
    in generations but still feel pushed
    like someone ranked in a succession.
It leaves me living in a time
    that's never ever time enough.
Imagine a clock with no hands
    but ticking flawlessly with utter

disregard for twelve irrelevant
numbers.
   Each tick's a heartbeat
long.
  That kind of time . . .

Itself

Beginnings end, but that's
  when endings just begin.
Take wars, for instance.
               They're
  waged again in books, in memory,
in monuments, in battlefields
preserved like parks.
               And that's
not all.
          Each death perpetuates,
but rarely truthfully, the life
it took.
          Which Washington do you
prefer?
          The father of his country
or the bald, false-toothed patrician
aging taciturn and childless
in Mount Vernon?
             History
supplies whatever preference
demands.
          But where's the benefit
and why?
          I'm drawn to anything
that has no life beyond its purpose.
Functional and equal to its task,
  it makes its end an ending
in itself.
          Once due, once used,
once prized for what it does
with no intended expectation

of reward or echo for posterity,
it meets its need like anything
that *is* before it *was.*
It could be sudden as a shooting
star, or simple as a shoelace.

Eyes

Startled like a girl surprised
   in her shower, the doe defied
   my stare.
              Animal to animal,
   we cancelled distance with our eyes.
For just that long I learned
   how much the present differs
   from presence.
              The present is
   what's here right now while
   presence is what's always here.
Lifting her foreleg to flee,
   the doe remained hoof-deep
   in shallows while we listened
   to each other with our eyes.
                 Fleet
   as an echo that lessens to nil,
   the listening lingered and lingered . . .
It's lingering still.
            That's presence.

5

The Dreams of Love

A Preferable Nudity

Goya's majas, for example . . .
The one in clothes would likely
    be ashamed unclothed.
                            The one
        that's nude would be defiled
        clothed.
                    This proves the naked
            and the nude are not the same.
A poem fraught with artifice
        before it's shorn of everything
        superfluous invites denuding
        from the start.
                            What's left at last
            might not be poetry at all.
A poem in the nude affirms
        its nudity without disguise.
It's absolute in all its spareness
        down to what defies
        addition or subtraction or indifference.
The maja in her finery and shoes
        presents a woman hidden
        by the muting camouflage of fashion.
The maja nude reveals
        a woman's total face
        in perpetuity unhidden and aloud
        from eyebrows down to toes.
Adornment would insult it.

The Art Professor Discusses Bernini's
Teresa in Ecstasy

Depicting her, Bernini did not sculpt
   the woman who would counsel popes
   or dance flamenco in the convent
   when the nuns were bored.
                          Instead,
   he focused solely on her face
   contorted in an agony of pleasure,
   her eyes half-lidded
   and her parted lips unwilling
   to return the oval of her mouth
   to silence.
              A bride outspread
   and straddling her lover's loins
   would look like this, her body
   primed for what she hopes will happen
   and desires more than breath
   itself.
           It's possible Bernini
   watched or fantasized a woman
   locked in such a wild tussle.
Why not transfer this image
   to a sainted nun?
                With consummation
   as his parable, Bernini carved Teresa
   swooning in God's orgy
   as any woman might when yielding
   to a love both wanton and permissible.

The Time It Takes to Tell

Posing *contrapposto* for the class,
    she seemed to say, "I'm here
    in body, but the rest of me
    is otherwhere."
               And why not?
Standing nude for minimum wage
    invites escape.
           Her breasts
and hips were fortyish, her pubes
    a darker auburn than her bangs,
    her appendectomy not quite obscure.
Regardless, the music of a woman's
    body sang in her, contained
    and hinted at like rubies in a purse.
Some of the student painters
    caught it on their canvases—echoes
    of de Milo or the shameless maja.
The model herself seemed unaware
    of what her body meant.
During a break she asked
    what time it was: "I never
    wear a watch at work because
    a watch would make me look
    not naked."
            I thought no more
of that as she resumed her role
    as Woman in the name of all
    her gender.
          Posed, her body
changed into a bet that said,
    "While the loser in me says

I just might win, the winner
tells me I could lose."
That seemed to leave her motionless
in mid-bet, shielded like a secret
in the sisterhood of female skin
while being re-created on a dozen
easels.
        The silence in the studio
was almost churchly.
                Later,
with the class dismissed and she
alone and bare, she found
her watch and strapped it on her wrist.
And just as suddenly as that,
    she seemed no longer naked.

Flagrante Delicto

Downriver from the Pont
du Gard while tourists parked
to picnic on the banks and benches,
and a multilingual guide explained
how arches of the aqueduct were built
with stones as old as Rome,
a woman and a man embraced
and grappled in the shelter of a cove
where they had hung their clothes
like laundry on an olive branch
until they fastened at the loins
and kept each other in a clasp
much older than a hundred Romes
in open view from the opposite
shore of a villa chosen
once by Richelieu for a visit
called official by its current
owners now in Avignon
just as their gardener, observing
totally by chance the doings
on the shore below, removed
his gloves to light his cigarette
and, braced against his planted
shovel, smoked and watched.

How Does Your Garden Grow?

No matter when I look
 at flowers, they're always saying
 hello.
             That's all they do.
Most repetitions bore me dull
 before they blur into annoyance:
 the way a barber's scissors
 never stops talking or how
 reverberating tides surrender
 in white murmurs to a shore.
But flowerbeds in bud or blossom
 thrive on repetition all their lives.
The more they bloom the more
 they seem to flourish in the blooming.
Some days I see them as defiant
 flags from all the countries
 of the world.
               On other days
 they look like brides and bridesmaids
 smiling for photographers and wanting
 nothing more than to be beautiful.

The Face of Catherine Deneuve

French without question—a smile
   that's nine parts mirth
   and one part doubt, the chin
   untucked and the left eyebrow
   arched a fraction.
                Never
a different face in public
   than in private, never a pose . . .
She sees whatever is there
   as if she's seen it twice
   too many times to be
   impressed.
             And that's what you
recall as you recall a French
   woman's way of dismissing nonsense
   with a click of her lips.
              In films
she's totally indifferent to how
   beautiful she is.
             It's not an act.
And there's no need for nudity
   to bare the woman within.
The face is nude enough
   to speak in every alphabet
   plus silence.
           Silence especially . . .
When someone noted that Deneuve
   had perfect features, a connoisseur
   from Montparnasse demurred
   with a smile, "Not perfect, but better."

Ophelia's Lie

Not that her innocence and age
    were an excuse . . .
                    After all,
    the girl could hold her own
    in argument, dispute her brother's
    platitudes and sing Elizabethan
    songs while strumming on a lute.
And she was beautiful as girls
    in adolescence are before they realize
    how beautiful they are.
                    What ended
    everything was when she let
    herself be used and then
    denied it to his face.
                    He never
    was the same . . .
                It took so little
    to destroy so much the way
    a microscopic but malignant speck
    can wreck a body, or a misprint
    maim a poem or a name.

6

Simply by Happening

To Be Continued: A Parable

It's like a play.
              Or rather
     the revival of a play in which
     you're still the main character.
The set, the lighting and the stage
     are what they were, but not
     the cast.
              Different actors
     have the roles that other actors
     acted when the play first
     ran.
              You make comparisons
     but then accept the differences
     as given.
              Somehow you only feel
     secure in character but alien
     to all the others on the stage.
Their names will keep on changing
     as the run resumes with younger
     people in older roles.
                        The script
     will stay the same.
                        You know
     your lines by heart but try
     to say them in a different voice
     each night.
              The other actors
     say your character and you
     are one.

Sometimes this seems
a sentence, sometimes a challenge.
Either way you keep on playing
your part.
You have no choice.

The Actor

My name is not important.
That's simply how I'm called,
  not who I am.
            I change
  from role to role on purpose.
Religious people claim
  you have to lose your life
  to find it.
            Actors do the same—
  true actors.
            It's not performance
  any more.
            It's transformation,
  and it's never simple.
            The man
  you shave and dress each day
  keeps getting in the way.
He wants you only as yourself—
  not thickened with another self,
  and then another, and another.
Every role demands a different
  way to die, and actors
  are in debt to dying.
            That's why
  I never married.
            No wife
  would ever understand.
            From time
  to time I find someone
  to share the solitude—someone
  to be caressed by and caress.

It makes things worse, but somehow
   truer.
          If there's a role
I'm offered that's for me, I go.
You'll always find me where I am
   as someone else.
                  Nowhere
but there.
          I have no address.

The Streetcorner Violinist

Under a movie marquee
   she slid the bow across
   the strings while passersby
   passed by.
               Few paused to listen.
Even fewer left a crumpled
   dollar in a baseball cap
   inverted for the purpose at her feet.
With both eyes shut she played
   something by Chopin.
               Perhaps
   a ticket charge for anyone
   inclined to listen might
   have guaranteed an audience,
   however small, since tickets
   always certify importance.
Unticketed, her solo seemed
   like something rendered in the key
   of beggary for alms.
               But if
   it was, it qualified as beggary
   with class.
            Amid the noise
   of shoppers' chatter, fumes
   from buses, auto horns and noise,
   one woman in a housedress
   played Chopin while no one
   listened, and the world spun on.
That seemed to me worth noting.

Sister Cigarette

She leans on her cane and smokes.
Her hair is Irish white.
She praised me once because
 I smoked a pipe the way
 her father did.
          "Pipe smokers
are never bad people," she said,
and flicked ashes.
          Sister
President could find no reason
to forbid what some considered
unbecoming for a nun near eighty.
That seemed divinely sensible.
On chill or sunny days she waves,
 and I wave back—like sailors
 on the decks of separate ships
 sailing in the same direction.

Big World, Little Girl

The poem in the photograph conceals
  itself.
      It's hidden in the perfect
overfloating clouds and less
than perfect trees whose branches
interrupt the sky.
        It hides
in little Sarah pausing
on a promenade of lawn surrounded
by space.
      And all at once
to your surprise, it's there.
         Who knows
what prompts a poem to reveal
itself the way that music
in performance can release
the secrets in the written score?
Clouds, trees, lawn
and little Sarah centered
in the shot . . .
      Click!
        And there's
the music.
     There's the poem.

Mary Anne with Camera

Your photographs of Czeslaw
   Milosz and Richmond Lattimore
   are good enough to be compared
   to portraiture by Karsh.
                    The same
   holds true for all your shots
   of Spanish doors or white-tailed
   deer beneath our backyard
   trellis.
          Your camera memorizes
   anything that lets itself be seen
   for a second, only.
                Timing
   and luck are important, but the lens
   is merely as good as its aim,
   and the aim's an art, and the art
   is rare.
          It takes all three
   to stop the world in passing
   long enough for it to gain
   a kind of immortality.
               That's
   what you do each time you hear
   a fraction of an instant say
   it's going, going, gone.
You and your camera say
   not now, not yet, not ever.

Sloth Is a Lost Art

You thought you'd take to menus
  à la carte with service, room
  and tax included in a prepaid
  package—and the Fahrenheit the same
  from day to day.
            You practiced
what believers call the virtue
of abandonment.
          And for a time
it helped.
      You totally forgot
what Brando's folly in Tahiti
prophesied.
      He bought an island
where he had the sea desalinated,
ordered what he ate flown in
and woke each day to propagate
the race.
      Short-lived as *Walden*
but less noble, the outcome
was the same.
        The sea sailed back
to salt, the dinners spoiled
in flight, and all the virgins
in Tahiti mated, mothered,
aged and in the process went
to fat . . .
    For you the change
was not as radical.
        Lounging
every day became a day

too long.
        You hungered for the phone
to ring.
        Monday was Thursday
was Sunday.
                Rest as a way
of life was hardly a match
for the Protestant ethic.
                        Moreover,
Eden without its snake became
a bore.

        It made you think
that boredom must have made
one apple seem more succulent
to Eve than usual.
                Or so
she dreamed.
                According to the myth,
our history began when Eve
succumbed to something tempting
on a whim.
                The choice was simpler
when it came to him.
                        Since he
had nothing much to think about
and no experience at all
with apples, consequence or women,
Adam bit.
                And that was it.

7

In the Name of Candor

No Words for This

If a true poem is one
   you wish you never had
   to write, then this is it.
Don't read it just to say
   you've read it.
            That's like
   the traveler who went to Spain
   so he could say he went
   to Spain.
           The words I've picked
   have really picked themselves,
   but what's not written here
   is where the poem breathes . . .
The mother of a captain killed
   by snipers read his final
   letter postmarked on the date
   he died.
         She read it often
after that.
         And every time
   she closed the envelope, she'd slowly
   lick it shut so that her tongue
   could taste him in the last
   thing he ever touched.

In the Fifth Year of the War

Saturday in Arlington.
                    Propping
    her crutch against a bench,
    a blonde unpockets her Nokia
    and takes a call that makes
    her laugh.
                    A man whose head
    is shaven glossy sleeps faceup
    on the grass, a half-read *Time*
    spread-eagled on his chest.
                            A girl
    with a star studded in one eyebrow
    strolls and waits for good news
    she hopes might happen.
                            The spaniel
    she tows on a leash decides
    she's been walked to wet, and wet
    she does in a female squat.
Two miles away the President
    of the United States is jogging
    the White House track
    with twin amputees.
                    Last week
    he addressed a sixth of his projected
    national audience.   .
                    He focused
    on "success" in one-fourteenth
    of all Iraq.
                    Later
    on cable a Marine sergeant
    described his Humvee's driver

after the ambush.
                    "He had
     his eyeball in his hand, and he
     kept trying to put it back in."
Still later a movie star
     was beeped when she blasphemed
     the war on its one thousandth
     six hundredth and forty-fourth day.

Riviera à la Carte

Let it be Tuesday on Cap
    Antibes.
                You wake to sun,
    hibiscus, royal palms
    and window-views of Nice
    and the Mediterranean Sea.
Later you surf the television
    news in English, French
    and Arabic: bombings in London
    and Lebanon, bloodletting in Iraq
    and sound-bites from a President
    known to speak daily to his staff
    and God on different frequencies.
You understand that news is always
    bad by definition, but still
    you can't not listen.
                Newspapers
    duplicate at breakfast everything
    you saw and heard on screen.
Intermingled with the smell of coffee
    and croissants, the mix becomes
    as scrambled as your eggs.
                You're faced
    with jumbled feasts for every
    appetite, and they are yours
    to eat.
        And so you read
    the eggs.
                You chew the news.

Skunked

Alamo, Great Wall or Maginot—
    they all were breached, bypassed
    or broken.
               Generals like Foch
condemned such barriers as futile
and extolled attack.
               But somehow
all attackers fail when conquests
burgeon into burdens, and the victims
mount rebellions and prevail.
Thucydides and Hemingway implied
    we're worse in war than beasts
    who only kill from need and never
    with malice.
               Are we that base?
Is strength the vice we copy
    from the lion?
               Guile from the fox?
Deception from the leopard?
               Stealth
    from the wolf?
               Or is this listing
too selective since it overlooks
the sane and self-reliant skunk?
He keeps his enemies at bay
    and stays untouched in the peace
    of the totally repugnant.

                    Cornered,
his odor scuttles the bother
of battle and shows the perceptive
few that stench is the perfect
weapon of choice for the bullied—
bloodless, inexpensive and effective.

Tell It to the Marines

While we philosophize, our headlines
    thrive on havoc—the grimmer
    the havoc, the larger and bolder
    the headlines.
                Though names and nations
    change, the bad news stays
    the same since half the governments
    on earth are run by murderers,
    elected or imposed.
              Camus
    believed that executions, wars
    and other legal murders
    were the cancers of our time.
                The headlines
    prove him right.
             But who
    still quotes Camus or thinks
    of Hammarskjöld or King or Kennedy
    as anything but memories?
              Their ends
    were violent, their legacies confined
    to anniversaries, their lives reduced
    to pages in unopened books
    or profiles minted on a coin.
And what is true of them
    is true as well of Gandhi, Lincoln,
    Thomas More and Socrates.
Why act indignant if the worst
    receive the best acclaim
    while all the most deserving end
    with none?

Given the choice
(before it's posthumous and safe
to do what they should earlier
and otherwise have done), the crowd
will choose Barabbas, ten to one.

Executioner

The guillotining blade was slanted
　　to permit a perfect slice.
You probably have seen engravings
　　where a bucket waits
　　to catch the severed head.
One wonders who the sadist was
　　behind this method of dispatch.
And by what God or government
　　commended?
　　　　　　In fact, a doctor—
Joseph Ignace Guillotin.
He thought beheadings merciful
　　compared to crucifixions, being
　　drawn and quartered, cracked
　　on a rack, roped to a post
　　and torched, or tugged to pieces
　　by horses.
　　　　　　He claimed a prisoner
　　would feel a feathery touch
　　at the nape of his neck, no more.
Gravity would do the rest.

Man Is the Only Animal Capable of Shame

Man is the beast with red cheeks.
Friedrich Nietzsche

I watched on film a pride
of lions feasting on a water
buffalo they'd overwhelmed.
They ripped
and clawed the carcass into shreds.
They cracked the bones.
Not one
was penitent.
Later they slept
or roamed or copulated in the open.
No matter what they did, they did it
in their naked skin and shamelessly.
Not us.
Consequence, not subsequence,
defines our lives, and consequences
mean that no one has the option
of impunity.
Our vices drive us
to addiction or repentance.
Killers,
liars, thieves and traitors
have been known to suffer genuine
remorse when facing their accusers.
This proves there still can be
contrition even from the worst.
Never to rollick like lions
in public, we're racked by appetites

and conscience, and the price for deviance
is guilt.
      Anguish returns us
to our suddenly awaiting
lives where we're still human
after all.
      What saves us
from the worst that we can be
but shame?
      What keeps us
always who we are but shame—
the merciless justice of shame?

Signs of Life in a Sundown City

We number less than half of what
  we were four decades back.
The young look elsewhere for their lives.
The old grow older and die.
Mansions of a long dead gentry
  calcify like skulls.
               Museums
lease from millionaires what artists
painted while they starved.
                   On streets
that once were prime, the smell
of oligarchy gone bourgeois is palpable.
The current synonym for blackjack,
  poker, craps and slots
is gaming.
          Uptown at midnight
the currency is drugs and guns,
and murderers grow younger
by the day.
          Regardless, the trees
parade in place at permanent
attention.
        Simply by happening,
each day proclaims itself unique
and unrepeatable.
         And two
undaunted rivers fork and fuse
into a third that flows into a fourth
that steers in silence to the sea
that's stayed the same since Genesis.

8

Between Two Shores

Prior to Oblivion

Even the totally forgettable
    forgets to be forgotten.
               Calling
    this regrettable but so, we live
    with echoes.
           How often have we
    fretted to recall a name,
    phone number or a face
    and come up blank?
             Since no one
    likes what's unacceptable, we blame
    the failure on fatigue or senioritis,
    but the cause is simpler than that.
Remembering four digits in a row
    is easy.
          Eleven is harder
    but possible.
             Forty's hopeless . . .
That's how it is with memory.
It chokes on gluttony and rids
    itself of dross by dumping
    the excess.
          If names and numbers
    vanish in the voiding, what's the loss?
Because the mind is made
    to make itself up and choose,
    the lesser trivia must go.
Knowing that the Great Wall
    of China is one thousand
    miles longer than America
    is wide is certainly of interest.

Noteworthy too that St. Augustine
  lived faithfully for nine years
  with the mother of his bastard son.
But these are facts, just facts.
If we remember everything
  that's past, we'll fatten with data
  or be sluiced away like flotsam
  in a flood.
          Summering hummingbirds
  know better.
          They flash through space
  in perfect symmetry.
          They savor
  only the important flowers.
The rest are noticed but ignored.
Why name the many or the few
  they favor?
          Better to stress
  how steadily they hover like tops
  kept spinning in place at full
  speed until they're ready
  to power down, ponder and choose.

Malaise

It happens when you feel as old
  as those too old to care
  how old they are.
                Bored
  with everything but breakfast,
  then sickened by the taste of toast,
  you take your coffee black—
  no sugar.
                This morning's headlines
  echo yestermorning's headlines
  to the letter.
                You read no further
  to remind yourself that news
  is never new.
                Each day is not
  a time to live but time
  to live through, and then
  not always as you like.
                The Germans
  have a word for this, as do
  the French, who have a word
  for everything.
                But then what
  difference does it make to give
  a name to what you feel
  in two or twenty languages?
It's simply there.
                It lingers
  like a stench that worsens by the day
  until one night, without
  a word or push from you,

105

it leaves as if it never
happened.
           You wonder if it's gone
for good or if it ever was.
Later you come to understand how
    you were wounded to the point
    of madness from within, although
    you stayed the man you are.
Compared to visible pain
    and anguish, this is not unusual.
Torturers proficient in the skills
    of malice have been known to leave
    their victims broken and babbling
    but unbloodied and without a scar.

In the Beginning Was the Breath

A Swedish linguist predicts
   the death of language itself,
   beginning with English.
                    Most
visions with apocalyptic endings
leave me cold, but not this one.
In his book called *Speak* he cites
   the disappearance of Sumerian
   as evidence.
                He hints that evolution
of the larynx, lungs and lips
might make unspeakable the words
we speak today.
                 As one
who lives from dawn to dusk
I'm leery of foretellings that require
eras to come true.
               It may be
otherwise in Sweden, but for me
all words are breaths.
                 If breath
and life are interchangeable,
then every sound we fashion
out of breath is simply life made
audible.
            It could be basic
as Greek, fluent as the Latin
sisters or the Indo-Europeans,
guttural as Finno-Ugric, plural
as Anglo-Saxon or diatonic
and curt as Arabic and Farsi.

They all were born from breath,
   just breath.
            And afterward they stayed
   alive in alphabets and books
   where memory survived long after
   talking had returned to silence.
To think of every tongue on earth
   extinguished like Sumerian or doomed
   by evolution seems too unforgiving
   a finale.
            Of course, a change
   could be much better than we think.
We all could draw our breaths
   in peace, and silence would become
   the universal language spoken
   only with the eyes.
                No one
   would have to bother with translations.
Babels would have no cause
   to tower to the sky.
                Everyone
   would speak the truth and be
   believed at sight because
   the eyes are too illiterate to lie.

Ars Poetica

I've had enough of poets
who repeatedly proclaim they're poets
or compose sestinas just to show
they can but never see that wordplay's
not the same as poetry, which matters
so much more since it confirms
that those who wield the pen
cannot help writing what they write
because the secrets that they learn
whenever they're inspired reveal
how poetry comes when it comes,
and when it comes, it comes
as unexpectedly as summer lightning,
and the few struck numb are dared
to say just once what only
rarely can be said at all,
but, dared or not, they strive
the way undaunted sculptors
carve and whittle masterpieces
out of ice although they're cautioned
in advance that warmer Fahrenheits
will swallow everything they sculpt
like substance silenced into shadow—
but still, but still they do it.

Poseidon and Others

His spear is somewhere sunk
  in the Aegean.
          The upraised hand
  grips nothing.
          His body's primed
for hurling—Olympian legs
astride, both shoulders squared,
the bearded face straightforward,
and the eyes aiming.
          Why quibble
if antiquities are flawed—a nose
chipped, a penis broken
at its base, a finger gone,
the arms of Aphrodite amputated
just beneath the shoulders?
          Flawless,
they would show us totally
what David offers us in Florence
to a fault.
          Even when complete
the statues of the Greeks revealed
the breasts of all the Caryatids
unnippled and the eyes opaque.
The wearing down of centuries
  would do the rest.
          Whipping
without his whip in hand,
the charioteer of Delphi rides
the wind.

The missing horse,
the whip, the chariot itself
have long since gone to ruin,
but the race that's never won
or lost has always just begun.

Home Are the Sailors

Like those who sail away and then
   come back, we keep returning
   to a port we've never left.
A life we used to live
   awaits us there as shores await
   all sailors home from sea.
So much is differently the same.
And yet what is the present
   but a future that the past
   made possible?
            There is
   no older story.
           And what
   are we but random pilgrims
   stopped in progress to remember?
It now seems more like then,
   why care?
           As long as home
   means where we most belong—
   for just that long—we're there.

Going

For Thomas Wolfe and Heraclitus
   time was a river flowing
   differently in place toward the sea.
They had a point.
                    A pair of shores
   divided by ongoing time
   is all the metaphor we need
   to show how permanence becomes
   impermanence until impermanence
   seems all that's permanent.
                            If that's
   the case, I have to ask
   if anything's preservable.
                        Or how?
Carthage and Troy are dust.
Aquinas ordered on his deathbed
   that his *Summa Theologica* be burned
   "as straw."
                    Likewise, my wish
   to see my three grandchildren
   grown is grudgingly improbable.
Why do I long for permanence
   when permanence is hopeless
   from the start?
                    I put this question
   to the river that I'm crossing now
   by bridge.
                    Insinuating westward
   to the Mississippi and finally
   the Gulf, the river says

the passing present is already
past.
      That tells me what
I must accept but hate
to know.
        I've lived this way
for years.
        No matter where
I go or when, I'm spanned
each day in permanent arrears
between two shores and bridging.